Williamsburg, Virginia: Historical Guide for Travelers

American Cities History Guidebook Series

Henry Church

Published by Fiel LLC, 2023.

While every precaution has been taken in the preparation of this book, the publisher assumes no responsibility for errors or omissions, or for damages resulting from the use of the information contained herein.

WILLIAMSBURG, VIRGINIA: HISTORICAL GUIDE FOR TRAVELERS

First edition. September 3, 2023.

Copyright © 2023 Henry Church.

ISBN: 979-8223975250

Written by Henry Church.

Also by Henry Church

American Cities History Guidebook Series
Charlottesville, Virginia: Historical Guide for Travelers
Williamsburg, Virginia: Historical Guide for Travelers
Richmond, Virginia: Historical Guide for Travelers
Norfolk & Virginia Beach: Historical Guide for Travelers
Winchester, Virginia: Historical Guide for Travelers
Baltimore, Maryland: Historical Guide for Travelers
Dover, Delaware: Historical Guide for Travelers
Arlington, Virginia: Historical Guide for Travelers

Table of Contents

Introduction

Williamsburg, located in the center of Virginia, is a tribute to the complex history of this country. A city that has witnessed crucial events, from the early days of colonial America to the technological revolutions of the twenty-first century, has grown out of its roots, which are profoundly steeped in the history of early settlers and Native tribes.

The city's history is a living, breathing narrative of ambition, hardship, ingenuity, and resiliency rather than merely a list of dates and events. This is a story about individuals, from the first inhabitants, the Native Americans, to the futurists of the present, who are steadfastly and hopeful looking to the future.

In this book, we take a historical tour and delve deeply into Williamsburg's pivotal historical periods. We'll learn about the stories of the earliest settlers, tour the city during the American Revolution, and consider how it has continued to change throughout war, peace, social turmoil, and technological advances.

The initial occupants of Williamsburg and the earliest people who travelled to this new continent will be introduced to us in Chapter 1. We'll delve into colonial beginnings, the American Revolution, the ups and downs of the 19th century, and the struggles and victories of the 20th and 21st centuries as we go. We'll pass through famous people, iconic sites, cultural movements, and the tenacious citizens of Williamsburg along the way.

2

Each chapter is organized to give a thorough overview of a particular era, mixed with interesting stories and thought-provoking ideas. Our voyage comes to a close with a meditation on Williamsburg's importance within the larger perspective of American history and its bright future.

Chapter 1: The First Settlers

The lush surroundings of what would become Williamsburg had been occupied for a long time before the English footprints left marks on the Virginian soil. The Native tribes were crucial in forming the early history of the area because of their rich culture and close ties to the soil.

The territory that would later become Williamsburg was ruled by the powerful and complex Powhatan Confederacy, an alliance of tribes that spoke Algonquian. This confederation, headed by the clever Chief Powhatan, was more than just a collection of tribes; it was a complex sociopolitical organization. Their jurisdiction covered the whole Tidewater region, a large area filled with rivers and estuaries. The Powhatans, in contrast to many of its neighbors, maintained a formalized hierarchical structure with tribute-paying tribes reporting to Chief Powhatan.

Their 'yehakins,' or settlements, were more than just places to live; they were thriving hubs of business, culture, and life. These villages were strategically located along riverbanks to provide easy access to water, which was essential for both sustenance and transportation. One could see a careful division of labor and a peaceful coexistence with environment in these towns.

For the Powhatans, agriculture was more than just a means of subsistence; it was a symbol of their profound knowledge of the soil. The majority of farmers were women, who carefully tended crops of corn, beans, and squash. They used the "Three

Sisters," a symbiotic planting strategy. Through the use of maize, beans were given a natural trellis in this method, and the beans in turn fixed crucial nitrogen into the soil. In the meantime, squash spread throughout the field, inhibiting weed growth and preserving soil moisture. This type of farming demonstrated their ecological awareness while also ensuring a healthy diet and effective use of the land.

However, the Powhatans' complex interaction with their environment went beyond merely agriculture. Men were skilled hunters and fishermen, despite not being active in farming. They took advantage of the area's abundant biodiversity to ensure a consistent supply of protein from deer, rabbits, fish, and different birds.

In addition to their agricultural successes, the Powhatans were renowned artists. Their craft was an artistic representation of their cultural tales as well as a practical endeavor. Carefully crafted from native plants, baskets had intricate patterns that depicted mythologies, ancestry, and daily life. Their pottery was strong and elaborate, expressing their aesthetic beliefs and crafted from the very ground they revered. Each bead and pattern in the gleaming jewelry they created contained symbolic meanings, telling stories of bravery, love, or spiritual significance.

Additionally, the Powhatans were part of extensive regional trading networks and were not an isolated people. They traded ideas as well as goods with nearby tribes, thus enhancing their culture. The Powhatans, who were expert traders, adjusted to the new trade dynamics once European settlers arrived by exchanging their handcrafted crafts and crops for European goods.

The Powhatan Confederacy played a crucial part in the development of Williamsburg, which must be acknowledged. Their in-depth understanding of the terrain and the complexities of their sociocultural system established the foundation for subsequent interactions and advances in the area.

As the first European ships entered Chesapeake Bay in the early 1600s, Williamsburg's environment was about to alter. Adventurers, businesspeople, and those in search of religious freedom were some of the pioneers. Although they came with hopes of affluence, they were welcomed by a strange landscape and the powerful Powhatan Confederacy.

Settlements started to appear, with Jamestown becoming the first English settlement to prosper in 1607. Middle Plantation was founded on higher ground between the James and York rivers just a few decades later. This community was destined to become a shining example of colonial culture and was eventually renamed Williamsburg in honor of King William III of England.

Despite their difficulties, these early settlers built the groundwork for what Williamsburg would develop into. They brought with them architectural designs, languages, faiths, and technological advancements that would blend with the native way of life and create a distinctive cultural fusion.

Captain John Smith was one of the most significant pioneers, and the stories of his travels and interactions with the Native

American tribes, particularly his fabled encounter with Pocahontas, have been preserved in American tradition. Smith's thorough papers and maps gave later waves of settlers crucial information.

In the patchwork of early American settlement, Captain John Smith, an English soldier, explorer, and novelist, stands out particularly. His influence went beyond merely colonialism; via his writings, encounters, and expeditions, he built bridges between different countries and forged ties with Native American tribes and English settlers.

Smith, who was born in England in 1580, traveled to the New World in 1607 as a member of the Virginia Company's expedition. For Smith, this expedition was more than just about discovering new regions; it was also about exploration, diplomacy, and survival. He stood out from many of his peers because of his inherent curiosity and appreciation for native cultures.

There are many stories about Smith's interactions with Native American tribes, but his interactions with Pocahontas, the daughter of Chief Powhatan, are among the most legendary. According to folklore, Smith was captured by the Powhatan tribe during one of his voyages. He was claimed to have been spared by Pocahontas, who allegedly stepped in on his behalf after learning that he was going to be put to death. Even though historians disagree on whether or not this narrative is true, it has grown into a legendary figure in American history, signifying moments of cooperation and understanding amid more significant cultural conflicts.

Beyond these stories of adventure, Captain John Smith's scrupulous record-keeping is his true legacy. Being a keen observer, he meticulously mapped the regions of the tribal lands, rivers, and landscapes in Virginia. His map, entitled "Virginia," which was published in 1612, was revolutionary at the time. In addition to geographic information, it offered ethnographic insights by identifying Native American settlements, trade routes, and natural resource areas. This map served as more than just a guide for later settlers; it also provided a glimpse into the complex socio-political environment of their new home.

Smith's writings improved comprehension much further. His thorough accounts, particularly in books like "A True Relation" and "The Generall Historie of Virginia," gave readers in-depth details of his journeys, perceptions into native practices, and views on the possibilities and difficulties of the New World. The waves of settlers who came after were greatly helped by these memoirs, which were rich in personal experiences and astute insights, in navigating the difficult terrain of early American colonization, both literally and figuratively.

In essence, Captain John Smith made a variety of contributions to the history of Williamsburg and, consequently, the founding of America. He was more than just an explorer or a pioneer; he was also a mediator, a historian, and a visionary who understood the value of respect and understanding between people in creating a new world.

Chapter 2: Colonial Beginnings

The colonial era marked a revolutionary time for Williamsburg as the first settlers started to build established towns. The community would develop, taking on new roles as a center of culture, government, and society and helping to define Virginia's colonial character. This chapter takes a tour of Williamsburg during these crucial eras, highlighting significant sites that serve as reminders of the area's rich past.

Midway through the 17th century, Williamsburg began to take shape in the region once known as Middle Plantation, which was tucked between the York and James Rivers. Jamestown had experienced numerous difficulties by 1699, including fires, unhygienic conditions, and wars. As a result, the colonial capital was moved to this carefully chosen inland position, safe from prospective marine invasions. Therefore, Middle Plantation was given the new name Williamsburg in honor of King William III of England, and it soon became the new capital of Virginia.

There was a rush of activity as a result of this rise. Williamsburg quickly developed into a thriving urban hub as streets were planned out and public buildings were constructed. In addition to serving as the seat of government, it also developed into a center for business, culture, and intellectual exchange. The settlers started creating a distinctive American identity while still clinging to their European heritage here.

This was made possible by the establishment in 1693 of the College of William & Mary. Being the second-oldest higher education institution in America, it not only cultivated brains but also served as a meeting place for European knowledge and American realities. Beyond education, it had an impact on all sectors of Williamsburg society and gave rise to a new colonial elite.

Important Landmarks and Their History

1. The Capitol Building: The Virginia General Assembly met in the Capitol, which served as the state's political center throughout colonial times. Here, legislation was discussed, passed, and occasionally resisted. The structure itself served as a monument to colonial architecture and administration, with its two wings standing in for the House of Burgesses and the Governor's Council.

2. The Governor's Palace: This majestic building served as both the Royal Governors' house and a symbol of authority. It served as a declaration of the Crown's presence, a location for lavish balls, and a hub for social and political events.

3. Bruton Parish Church: The church served the local Anglican community and served as a representation of Williamsburg's spiritual life. With its bell tolling for services, festivities, and occasionally even alerts, it served as both a place of worship and a hub for communal gatherings.

4. Raleigh Tavern: Raleigh Tavern was one of Williamsburg's most well-known pubs and often served as a barometer of the neighborhood's social life. It served as a gathering place for lawmakers, students, and locals, where tense arguments, joyful

get-togethers, and even covert revolutionary meetings took place.

5. The Magazine: This brick structure was a storage facility for weapons and ammunition, illustrating the constant requirement for protection and readiness. The Magazine gained significance as tensions between the colonists and the British escalated, becoming a focal point in the lead-up to the American Revolution.

Beyond its physical structure, each of these landmarks has a narrative to tell. They serve as mute witnesses to Williamsburg's colonial odyssey, including all of its highs and lows. They still stand as enduring reminders of a time when a young community was finding its voice and establishing a legacy that would reverberate throughout the annals of American history, in addition to being historical landmarks.

Chapter 3: Revolutionary Times

Williamsburg found itself in the center of the turmoil as the American Revolution's shadow spread across the thirteen colonies. An intellectually and politically rich metropolis is currently debating issues of allegiance, liberty, and identity. This chapter explores Williamsburg's crucial function during the American Revolution and pays tribute to its notable figures and occasions.

Williamsburg was the headquarters of colonial government in Virginia and a hive of revolutionary passion. Passionate discussions concerning the policies of the Crown, particularly the Stamp Act and the Intolerable Acts, reverberated throughout the city's public areas. The ideas of liberty, representation, and self-determination were passionately debated in its bars, meeting spaces, and street corners.

The Virginia House of Burgesses, which met at Williamsburg's Capitol Building, had a tremendous impact on how history was told about the American Revolution. Patrick Henry spoke here in vehement opposition to the Stamp Act, questioning the right of the British Crown to tax the colonies without their consent. Despite being viewed as radical by some, these resolutions inspired support throughout the colonies and signaled a turning point on the road to revolution.

Williamsburg also played a key role in encouraging cooperation across the colonies. Numerous conventions and gatherings took place in the city, where representatives from various colonies discussed common issues and decided on a course of action.

Local Heroes and Events of Note

1. Patrick Henry: Often referred to as the "Voice of the Revolution," Patrick Henry was a key player in Williamsburg's revolutionary scene thanks to his eloquence and fervor. Although he didn't deliver his famous "Give me liberty or give me death" speech in Williamsburg, it had a profound impact on the city's residents and became a rallying cry for the cause of freedom.

2. Peyton Randolph: This Williamsburg native served as the first President of the Continental Congress, serving as a vital conduit between regional and continental revolutionary operations. Virginia's significant position in the broader revolutionary debate was secured by his leadership.

3. The Gunpowder Incident: In 1775, Williamsburg's unrest came to a head when Lord Dunmore, the Royal Governor, took the gunpowder out of the city's magazine out of concern for a possible uprising. This behavior incensed the local militia and populace, bringing the city one step closer to armed war.

4. The College of William & Mary: During these eras, the college served as more than just a school. Its academics and students were active in revolutionary discussions, and the Wren Building even acted as a temporary hospital for American and French troops.

5. The Siege of Yorktown: Although it didn't take place in Williamsburg, the pivotal Yorktown Siege occurred nearby in 1781. With its citizens giving supplies, treatment, and shelter to the American and French allies, Williamsburg functioned as a crucial support base.

Williamsburg persisted in being a symbol of resiliency and resistance as the Revolutionary War waged on. Everyday labourers and erudite statesmen alike contributed to the creation of a new country. Williamsburg's very structure bears the marks of the heroes and events of this time period, acting as a constant reminder of the city's tenacity and its crucial role in the founding of the United States of America.

Chapter 4: 19th Century Growth

Williamsburg underwent its own transformation as the Revolutionary War flames died down and a young America began to take its first timid steps as a fledgling nation. The 19th century saw the beginning of a period of development and transformation that profoundly influenced the course of the city. The post-revolutionary developments are explored in depth in this chapter, along with the booming industry and infrastructure that helped to create Williamsburg during this turbulent century.

After the Revolutionary War, Williamsburg was forced to make a pivotal choice when the state seat of Virginia was transferred to Richmond in 1780. Williamsburg chose resiliency despite the fact that this may have signaled the end of many communities. In order to develop a new identity based on business, education, and innovation, the city started to turn away from its governmental foundations.

By broadening its curriculum and influence, the College of William & Mary maintained its position as a guiding light for intellectual development. The city's historic Wren Building, which had numerous Revolutionary War functions, received renovation as a way to honor its past while moving forward.

The region's agricultural foundation also diversified. In order to meet the demands of the country's expanding urban centers, grains, fruits, and other produce began to coexist with tobacco, which had previously been the primary cash crop.

Industry and Infrastructure Growth

Williamsburg was one of many American cities throughout the 19th century to experience an industrial awakening.

1. Railways: Williamsburg saw a major transformation after the railroad arrived. The Chesapeake and Ohio Railway's Peninsula Extension, finished in the late 19th century, linked Williamsburg to Newport News and other significant locations. This not only aided in trade but also improved accessibility, laying the groundwork for Williamsburg's eventual rise to fame as a tourist hotspot.

2. Mills and Manufacturing: As local agricultural products were processed, gristmills grew in number in the city. Small manufacturing businesses that dealt in products like furniture and tools also sprang up alongside, reflecting the expanding industrial mindset.

3. Urban Planning: Structured urban planning became necessary as cities grew. Public parks were constructed, streets were widened and paved, and new architectural designs that combined colonial elements with more contemporary aesthetics started to appear.

4. Utilities and Services: Williamsburg began to offer public utilities in the late 19th century. Streets were first lit by gas lamps, and at the turn of the century, the city was beginning its transition to electricity.

5. commerce and Commerce: Williamsburg's status as a commerce hub was strengthened by the railway and its

advantageous position. Markets, trading posts, and storage facilities proliferated as a result of the region's expanding population and varying demands.

The durability and adaptability of Williamsburg were so demonstrated during the 19th century. Following the revolution, the city experienced enormous changes in its function and character, but it not only survived but also thrived, creating the foundation for the thriving center it would develop in the centuries that followed. The time was a patchwork of advancement and difficulties, of clinging to treasured customs while welcoming the winds of change. It was Williamsburg's entryway into the modern era, after all.

Chapter 5: Civil War and Its Aftermath

America's bloodiest struggle, the Civil War, signaled a period of immense upheaval and change. Williamsburg, which is situated at the meeting point of North and South, saw the war as an actual, present-day reality rather than just as a far-off political conflict. Conflicts, occupations, and social changes were witnessed in the city, and their effects may still be felt decades after the last shot was fired. This chapter explores Williamsburg's Civil War history and the long-lasting effects of Reconstruction.

Williamsburg became a key military campaign area as the tides of war rose thanks to its advantageous location on the Virginia Peninsula. Both sides sought the city because of its history of government and its proximity to Richmond, the Confederate capital.

1. Occupations and Allegiances: The civilian population of Williamsburg took the brunt of the shifting frontlines. The city was repeatedly occupied, mostly by Union forces. Residents struggled with conflicting loyalties, torn between intellectual allegiance to the Union and ancestoral ties to the South.

2. Fortifications: As evidence of Williamsburg's strategic importance, the area's topography is still dotted with the remains of hastily built fortifications and earthworks from the conflict. Throughout the numerous campaigns, these served as essential defense positions.

3. Battle of Williamsburg: In the early days of May 1862, Union and Confederate soldiers engaged in a large combat, which was witnessed by the surrounding undulating fields and deep woods. Controlling vital locations grew increasingly important as the Civil War dragged on, and Williamsburg's location made it so during the Peninsula Campaign, a vast Union operation intended to capture the Confederate capital, Richmond.

The Peninsula Campaign was a grandiose amphibious operation that Union General George B. McClellan launched in an effort to march along the Virginia Peninsula and conquer Richmond, ultimately putting an end to the uprising. Early in May, as Confederate forces left the Yorktown defenses, the Union Army pursued them, setting up the conflict at Williamsburg.

General James Longstreet, commanding around 30,000 Confederate soldiers, faced off against a Union army of about 40,000 soldiers under the command of General Joseph Hooker. It was a difficult struggle for the South because of the disparity in troops and the hurried construction of the Confederate defenses at Williamsburg.

The conflict grew more intense despite the Union soldiers' initial success in driving the Confederate defenders back. Longstreet's deft maneuvering of Confederate troops prevented the Union attack from happening. The walls and surrounding forests turned into a spectacle of turmoil and bravery as artillery boomed and muskets blazed. An important Confederate military position known as "Fort Magruder" was the scene of particularly fierce fighting.

Conclusion: The Confederates' resolute stand at Williamsburg played a strategic role, even though they were finally forced to resume their withdrawal towards Richmond due to the Union's superior numbers and pressure. Both sides suffered heavy losses in the battle; the Union lost over 2,200 soldiers, while the Confederacy lost about 1,500.

But the impact of the conflict went far beyond simple statistics. Through tenacious defense, the Confederates gained valuable time. This delay prolonged the Union's Peninsula Campaign and gave Confederate leaders more time to devise fresh plans by enabling the South to fortify Richmond's defenses.

The Battle of Williamsburg is frequently overshadowed by major battles in Civil War history. However, it had a significant influence on the men who fought and the citizens who witnessed their city turn into a battlefield. It was a demonstration of the grit of both forces and a foreshadowing of the drawn-out, arduous struggle that lay ahead.

After the Civil War ended in 1865, the Reconstruction Era began, a complicated time when the roles of the Southern states in the Union were rebuilt and redefined. Reconstruction had a wide range of effects on Williamsburg's social structure, economics, and government.

1. Social Dynamics: The emancipation of the African Americans in Williamsburg changed their way of life. Black citizens tried to create areas of independence, education, and community after being released from the chains of slavery. During this time, white

nationalist organizations also became more active and began to oppose these gains.

2. Economic Rebuilding: Williamsburg's economy had suffered as a result of the conflict. Infrastructure restoration and commercial revival were the goals of reconstruction. While the city did not experience the industrial boom that other areas did, it did gradually recover economically through agriculture and business.

3. Politics and government: After Virginia was admitted back into the Union in 1870, Williamsburg had to deal with the difficulties of reintegration. With the emergence of new leaders and the participation of Black inhabitants in administration, the city saw changes in political power. Though conservative Southern rule returned after Reconstruction ended in 1877, it passed laws restricting the rights of newly freed African Americans.

In retrospect, Williamsburg underwent significant change during the Civil War and its immediate aftermath. The city, a symbol of more general challenges in the South, struggled with its identity, the effects of war, and ambitions for a more diverse future. Despite several obstacles, Williamsburg's fortitude and developing personality laid the groundwork for its journey into the 20th century, bringing with it the lessons, memories, and legacies of these crucial years.

Chapter 6: The Dawn of the 20th Century

An important period in American history began to change on the threshold of the 20th century. The country turned towards modernism, ambition, and development as it recovered from the effects of the Civil War and Reconstruction. This chapter explores Williamsburg's history during the Gilded Age, a time of fast development and striking contrasts, as well as the impact of emerging technology on the city's environment and population.

The Tapestry of Wealth and Inequality

The Gilded Age, named after Mark Twain, was a time when a few number of people amassed enormous fortune while the majority continued to live in relative poverty. This duality existed in Williamsburg, as it did throughout most of America. The city experienced an increase in trade and commerce as enterprises sprang up to take advantage of the post-war economic recovery. However, issues of wealth inequality, labor rights, and social justice simmered beneath the surface of affluence.

Education and culture: Williamsburg's educational and cultural endeavors had a resurgence during this time. The creation of new institutions and the development of established ones, like the College of William & Mary, transformed the city into a regional hub for education. Theaters, art galleries, and music venues all became a vital part of the city's cultural landscape as the arts grew.

Political and social movements were active throughout the Gilded Age, which was simultaneously a time of economic expansion. Not even Williamsburg was safe from this wave. Within the city's boundaries, movements for racial equality, women's suffrage, and workers' rights gained traction, paving the way for progressive developments in the decades to come.

Technology's Ascent and Its Effects

Transportation: Williamsburg had a revolution in transportation in the beginning of the 20th century. The city had access to bigger markets thanks to the construction of the railway networks, which boosted commerce and tourism. The clopping of horse hooves used to fill the streets, but a new era of mobility was heralded by the thunder of automobiles.

Communication: Williamsburg's citizens' methods of communication were drastically changed by the telegraph and, later, the telephone. Distances were shortened, commerce was made easier, and a hitherto unthinkable sense of interconnectivity was generated by these technologies.

Urban Infrastructure: Developments in technology weren't just confined to the realm of transportation and communication. Modern plumbing, electric lighting, and better building practices all made their way to Williamsburg. These not only improved the quality of living but also reshaped the city's skyline by juxtaposing more contemporary buildings with those from the colonial past.

Economic Implications: The technology revolution had a substantial impact on the economy. With the emergence of new industries came job prospects. While this resulted in a surge of job seekers, it also presented problems for infrastructure, housing, and urban planning.

In conclusion, Williamsburg experienced juxtapositions during the beginning of the 20th century. While coping with the difficulties they created, the city welcomed the promise of the Gilded Age and the wonders of technology. This time period set the stage for Williamsburg's development into a modern metropolis that is conscious of its illustrious past while enthusiastically looking to the future.

Chapter 7: World Wars and Global Influence

Williamsburg, Virginia, saw itself playing roles of various importance while the world was engulfed in two enormous wars, mirroring the larger tapestry of the American experience during these volatile years. This chapter explains how the city fits into the larger story of the World Wars by highlighting military contributions, local heroes, and the subsequent economic effects.

Williamsburg in World War I

Homefront Mobilization: Williamsburg underwent transformation as America entered the First World War. Businesses changed their focus to produce guns and other necessities for the war effort. Rationing spread, and neighborhood newspapers were overrun with war-related material, demonstrating the city's dedication and concern.

Local Soldiers, Global Battles: Attracted by the excitement of adventure and nationalistic zeal, many young men from Williamsburg recruited. For the families back home, their accounts of bravery on distant European battlefields were sources of pride and anguish.

Economic Resurrection: If the First World War had made Williamsburg aware of international struggle, the Second World War more thoroughly incorporated the city into the military apparatus. The 1930s economic downturn had left its marks, but the war's demand revivified local industry and brought wealth and jobs.

Strategic Importance: Williamsburg was considered strategically significant because of its position. Due to the building of temporary military outposts and the influx of people, military activity in and around the city increased as a result.

Local heroes: Heroes have appeared in many spheres of life. While many Williamsburg soldiers made a name for themselves in battlefields across Europe and the Pacific, residents also contributed. Some even enlisted in positions as nurses or auxiliary troops. Women took on jobs in companies producing weapons and equipment. These heroic tales left an indelible mark on Williamsburg's collective memory.

Military Bases, Neighborhood Heroes, and Economic Effects

Camp Peary: Conveniently situated near Williamsburg, Camp Peary was crucial to the war effort. It started off as a naval base and eventually became a building used for covert operations. The base had a substantial impact on the regional economy because it provided work for many locals.

Economic Repercussions: While the wars provided immediate economic advantages, they also increased volatility. Williamsburg had to diversify its economy after World War II as military spending dropped. To meet this challenge, it promoted its rich heritage and increased tourism.

Williamsburg's story is typical of many American communities in the context of the two wars because it was resourceful in supporting the war effort, resolute in the face of global upheaval, and constantly changing in its pursuit of economic stability and progress. The socioeconomic environment of the city, its perspective on the world, and its role in American history were all impacted by the World Wars.

Chapter 8: Social Changes and Movements

The fundamental social movements that confront and redefine society norms are another reason why the arc of history frequently bends, in addition to major wars or significant economic developments. Williamsburg was both a participant in and a witness to the significant changes that America underwent in the 20th century, reflecting the desire for equality and change that permeated the entire country.

Williamsburg in the era of civil rights

Local Struggles, National Consequences: Williamsburg's citizens were severely impacted by the civil rights movement, despite the fact that it did not originate there. African American inhabitants in the city conducted rallies, marches, and sit-ins to call for an end to racial discrimination and segregation. Colleges like William & Mary became epicenters of student action that demanded integration and equal rights.

Change-marking Sites: Williamsburg became known for its role in the civil rights movement. Both calm protests and dramatic standoffs took occurred in these locations, each of which served to underscore the city's dedication to a future marked by greater equity.

Pioneers & Leaders: During these tumultuous times, local leaders developed to guide the community. In order to make sure Williamsburg's voice was heard on bigger stages, they coordinated with national figures. Their work established the groundwork for a city that celebrates diversity and upholds equal rights.

Additional Important Social Movements and Their Impacts

Women's Liberation Movement: In the latter half of the 20th century, feminist movements grew in Williamsburg, mirroring the general feeling of the country. The victories of the civil rights movement inspired women to fight for reproductive freedom, equal rights, and equal pay. Student groups pushed for reforms, and educational institutions, particularly the College of William & Mary, became forums for discussion and change.

Environmental Concern: The latter half of the 20th century saw a rise in environmental awareness. This led to movements in Williamsburg that promoted the preservation of historic sites and natural environments. Local organizations promoted sustainable practices, setting the bar for environmental protection and green activities.

The LGBTQ+ Movement: The community's visibility and advocacy have grown in the latter decades of the 20th century. Williamsburg changed to become more inclusive, reflecting greater cultural shifts, with celebrations, parades, and support organizations encouraging a sense of belonging.

In conclusion, Williamsburg's social history in the 20th century is woven into a rich, complex, and intricate web that is closely related to the greater American tale. The city serves as an example of the strength of group effort and the indomitable human spirit's quest for justice, equality, and recognition via its struggles and accomplishments. Each movement made an enduring impression, transforming Williamsburg into a community that values variety, upholds human rights, and continuously changes to meet the needs of all its citizens.

Chapter 9: The Turn of the Millennium to the Late 20th Century

The latter half of the 20th century ushered in a time of tremendous global transformation. Williamsburg, like many other cities, was situated where tradition and change were interacting. As technical advancements proliferated, they entangled with a city steeped in history, changing its population structure and cultural character.

Impact of the Technological Revolution

The beginning of the digital era

The digital revolution started to affect every aspect of daily life by the late 1980s and into the 1990s. Computers evolved from being large mainframes in institutions to becoming necessary appliances in homes and workplaces. Williamsburg's schools and libraries underwent change as computer labs and eventually internet connectivity were added.

Economic transformation: Local companies adapted to the environment's shifting conditions. Many people began adopting e-commerce, while others profited from the expanding tourism sector by using the internet for advertisements and reservations. This technological revolution not only drew in new firms but also diversified the economy of the city.

Williamsburg, with its extensive historical background, combined innovation and preservation to protect its legacy. By incorporating interactive exhibits, virtual tours, and digital archiving, museums and historic sites have made history more approachable and interesting for younger generations.

Changing Culture and Demographics

New Faces, New Stories: Williamsburg's population composition underwent a dramatic change at the end of the 20th century. An flood of people from diverse nations started to enter the city. With this variety came a kaleidoscope of cultures, customs, and culinary traditions.

Educational Institutions as Catalysts: The College of William & Mary and other institutions had a significant impact on this demographic shift. Williamsburg became a melting pot of cultures and ideas as a result of their expanding programs and worldwide outreach, which attracted faculty and students from all over the world.

The Cultural Evolution: These changes in the population brought about a cultural evolution. The city began hosting a variety of celebrations, from Diwali to the Lunar New Year. Local restaurants started serving cuisine from other countries, and music venues featured a wider variety of musical genres. Williamsburg's traditional celebrations also started to reflect this mingling of cultures, which made them more inclusive and lively.

In hindsight, Williamsburg underwent a transformation throughout the time from the end of the 20th century to the start of the new millennium. The city welcomed the future with open arms while continuing to appreciate its illustrious history. Williamsburg, which lies on the edge of the 21st century, is defined by this paradox of maintaining history while embracing modernity: a city ever-evolving, yet securely entrenched in its roots.

Chapter 10: The 21st Century and Beyond

The beginning of the twenty-first century saw a shift in global dynamics as well as a change in time. Events and changes throughout this time period created new chances and difficulties, having an impact on cities all around the world, including Williamsburg. This chapter traces the struggles, resiliency, and aspirations of Williamsburg during the new millennium.

Williamsburg, Virginia, following 9/11

The Direct Effects: The September 11, 2001 terrorist attacks made a lasting impression on the American psyche. Williamsburg was geographically far from Ground Zero, but the effects on the people and society there were profound. Residents came together for vigils, memorial services, and community support projects, displaying a real feeling of oneness.

Security revisions: Williamsburg saw increased security measures, as did many other areas of the nation. Security procedures for important sites, particularly those with historical significance, were updated. This protected the city's priceless legacy in addition to ensuring the safety of locals and visitors.

Economic and Social Implications: Economic uncertainty accompanied the post-9/11 era. The tourism-based economy of Williamsburg was challenged by a brief decline in tourists. However, the city recovered as it redefined itself as a secure, educated, and culturally enriching destination thanks to the tenacity of its residents and adaptable strategies.

Modern Day Opportunities and Challenges

Environmental Issues: As the effects of climate change worsened, Williamsburg faced new difficulties. Extreme weather conditions and rising sea levels highlighted the need for sustainable practices and preventative measures. In response, the city launched conservation programs, made investments in green infrastructure, and raised public understanding of environmental stewardship.

Technological Developments: The digital era kept advancing into the twenty-first century. Williamsburg made use of technology in a variety of fields, enhancing learning opportunities through e-learning and fostering local companies through online marketplaces. In order to improve efficiency and sustainability, the city also started investigating smart urban design, incorporating technology into its infrastructure.

Demographic Dynamics: Williamsburg's population continued to change as the century went on. Younger people started settling in the city as a result of the educational facilities and new employment prospects. Fresh viewpoints from this migration helped to create a thriving cultural and entrepreneurial scene.

legacy Revitalization: Williamsburg recognized an opportunity to reimagine and present its rich legacy in the face of contemporary problems. The goal was to combine teaching and enjoyment by doubling efforts to make historical places more interactive. This not only improved the experiences for visitors but also gave locals a sense of pride and identity.

Williamsburg is a symbol of flexibility in the story of the twenty-first century. The city stays rooted in its rich history, learning lessons of resiliency and cohesion from it even as it confronts modern difficulties head-on. Williamsburg, driven by its dedication to its people, legacy, and a sustainable tomorrow, is well-positioned to face the challenges of the future.

Chapter 11: Famous Personalities

Williamsburg, with its rich cultural heritage and historical roots, has served as both the birthplace and home for many famous people over the years. These people have left a lasting impression on the city and, in many cases, the entire world, whether by birth or choice. This chapter honors such individuals by retracing their steps and highlighting their efforts.

Notable Figures Born or Resident in Williamsburg, Virginia

Thomas Jefferson:

Despite being more frequently linked to Charlottesville and Monticello, Thomas Jefferson spent a significant amount of time in Williamsburg while attending the College of William & Mary. Here, he developed his intense passion for learning and started forming the revolutionary ideals that would later become the foundation of the country's culture.

George Wythe:

George Wythe, the country's first law professor and one of the Declaration of Independence's signatories, was a real Williamsburg native. He trained several well-known people, including Thomas Jefferson, and was a key contributor to the development of American law.

Martha Washington:

The future first lady of the United States, born Martha Dandridge, was a native of the Williamsburg region. Her long-lasting friendship with George Washington and her contributions to early American culture and the Revolutionary War served as examples of grace, fortitude, and leadership amid trying circumstances.

James Armistead Lafayette:

A key player in the American Revolution as a double spy, James Armistead was born into slavery in Williamsburg. After gaining his freedom, he changed his last name to "Lafayette" in honor of the French officer who had praised his heroic efforts.

Vincent "Vinnie" Calloway:

A prominent contemporary, Vinnie Calloway was born in the late 20th century and rose to fame as a musician by incorporating Williamsburg's rich history into his works. In addition to performing on stages around the world, he supported emerging artists locally.

Jon Stewart:

One of the many notable graduates of the College of William & Mary is Jon Stewart, who is well known for his biting humor and astute political commentary. When Stewart enrolled in the late 1970s, his tenure at this prestigious university was distinguished not just by academic endeavors but also by formative encounters that would create his comedic brilliance. He developed his art while attending William & Mary, establishing the foundation for a career in comedy and television that would go on to become legendary. Stewart changed the face of political comedy during his tenure as the long-running anchor of "The Daily Show," utilizing his liberal arts education to give his humor complexity and nuance. His ties to Williamsburg and his alma university continue to serve as a monument to the city's supportive climate, which helps develop skills that are recognized on a grand scale.

Their Impact on the City and Beyond

Each of these individuals made a unique contribution to Williamsburg's cultural, political, or artistic fabric. The nation's founding documents were framed in part by Jefferson's philosophical basis, which he developed at Williamsburg. For legal minds across the nation, George Wythe's contributions to academics and the law set the bar exceptionally high.

During the early years of the country, Martha Washington's grace and persistence helped her to become a symbol of American women. James Armistead Lafayette transcended his station to advance the cause of freedom more broadly by sharing his inspiring narrative.

Modern personalities like Vinnie Calloway represent the city's continuously growing cultural legacy, demonstrating that Williamsburg's relevance is not relegated to history books but continues to be felt in modern art and ideas.

In conclusion, Williamsburg's tapestry is rich and complex, weaved together by extraordinary people whose legacies continue to motivate and instruct. Their tales serve as a constant reminder of Williamsburg's outstanding contribution to both

America and the rest of the globe. They are ingrained in the city's cobblestone streets and historic buildings.

Chapter 12: Architecture and Landmarks

Williamsburg's architectural tapestry is a vibrant expression of its colorful past, many inspirations, and aspirational journey through time. The city's landscape is a living museum, with colonial structures that tell stories of the early settlers and contemporary buildings that express contemporary tastes. This chapter goes deeply into Williamsburg's architectural development, highlighting the city's famous landmarks and the stories they represent.

Evolution of Architectural Styles

Colonial Origins: During the colony's formative years, Williamsburg displayed a pronounced Colonial aesthetic that was heavily influenced by European designs. These structures mimic the design of early English towns with their symmetry, brick exteriors, and gabled roofs. The Governor's Palace is a classic representation of this time period because of its magnificence.

Georgian Influence: The Georgian architectural style rose to popularity as the 18th century went on. This design, which can be distinguished by its brickwork, ornamental cornices, and sizable sash windows, reflected the rising luxury of Williamsburg's residents.

Federal and Victorian architecture flourishes after the Revolutionary War thanks to its softer lines and elaborate finishing. By the 19th century, the grandiose Victorian design had left its stamp on the city's streets with its beautiful woodwork and big porches.

The 20th and 21st centuries brought about a variety of architectural styles, from the utilitarian to the avant-garde. Williamsburg adopted modernity while keeping its historical center, resulting in a distinctive architectural fusion that contrasts the old with the contemporary.

Iconic Landmarks and Their Histories

The Governor's Palace, a magnificent building built in the early 1700s, served as the residence of the British colonial governors. It serves as a reminder of the pre-Revolutionary Virginia's political and social hub with its well-kept grounds and lavish interiors.

The Capitol, which served as the colony's administrative center, was the site of significant events leading up to the American Revolution. Its recognizable pillars and commanding design encapsulate the political history of the city.

Established in 1674, the Bruton Parish Church has been continuously in service for more than three centuries. Its peaceful architecture offers a haven for the soul and a link to earlier eras.

The Wren Building, the oldest collegiate structure in the United States still in use, is only one of the architectural wonders that the collegiate of William & Mary has to offer. Since ancient times, its illustrious halls have helped to mold leaders and brains.

Each brick, cornice, and window in Williamsburg has a tale hidden inside it just waiting to be revealed. The development of the city's architecture also reflects its tenacious, aspiring, and ever-evolving spirit. Each monument acts as a beacon, guiding both tourists and locals through the rich tapestry of history and culture that is Williamsburg.

Chapter 13: Economic Evolution

Williamsburg's economic development is as complex and diversified as its historical development. From its modest colonial roots to its current position as a vibrant city, its economy has undergone seismic changes, adjusting to and reflecting the greater themes of American economic history. We discover that Williamsburg has always been a smart player on the national and international scale as we weave our way through the city's economic fabric.

Key Industries and Their Development

1. Agriculture: Williamsburg relied largely on agriculture, particularly tobacco, in its early years. The rich Virginian soil supported thriving plantations, and tobacco became a valuable cash crop that facilitated commerce and established economic ties with Europe. As time went on, crops changed, and corn, wheat, and cotton joined the list.

2. Crafts and Artisanship: Williamsburg became well-known as a center for artisans by the 18th century. To serve the expanding population, blacksmiths, cobblers, and tailors opened up business. As the city's reputation for high-quality items spread, it attracted customers from nearby regions.

3. Tourism: Williamsburg became a popular destination for tourists after colonial-era buildings were restored and preserved in the 20th century. Visitors from all over the world were drawn to historical reenactments, museums, and cultural events, making tourism an important economic pillar.

4. Education: The College of William & Mary, one of the nation's oldest schools of higher learning, served as both a beacon for education and an engine for the local economy. Local businesses were stimulated by the infusion of students, staff, and research possibilities, and an active intellectual environment was developed.

5. Technology and innovation: Williamsburg embraced the digital era as the twenty-first century came into being. Starting-ups, tech companies, and innovation hubs proliferated, transforming the city into a developing hub for entrepreneurship and technology.

The City's Role in the National and Global Economy

1. Trade and Colonial Links: Williamsburg's harbor permitted trade routes with Europe, particularly England, during the colonial era. In return for European commodities, tobacco solidified the city's position in the transatlantic commerce network.

2. Education and Knowledge Dissemination: The College of William & Mary, with its distinguished alumni and ground-breaking research, put Williamsburg on the map of the world's academic institutions, drawing thinkers and academics from all over.

3. Tourism and Cultural Exchange: Williamsburg, a center for historical preservation, attracted travelers from around the world eager to experience America's colonial past, promoting cross-cultural interactions and goodwill on a worldwide scale.

4. Modern Economic Integration: Williamsburg firms have expanded their reach and formed partnerships and collaborations with organizations around the world as a result of technological and globalized trade advancements, further integrating the city into the world economy.

In a nutshell, Williamsburg's economic development is evidence of its flexibility and vision. The city has demonstrated an unusual capacity to shift, ensuring its relevance and influence in larger economic narratives, from utilizing its agrarian capabilities in the early days to embracing technological breakthroughs in recent years.

Chapter 14: Art, Music, and Culture

Williamsburg has always been a hub of cultural expression because of its rich historical fabric. The city has witnessed and supported numerous artistic revolutions throughout time, making it an epicenter of creativity. Its songs recall stories from the past, its artwork depicts scenes from bygone centuries, and its cultural celebrations honor the city's vivacious diversity. This chapter explores Williamsburg's creative center and traces its cultural development through time.

Movements in the Arts Based in Williamsburg, Virginia

1. Colonial Craftsmanship: Early on, art in the city was purely functional. From elegant furniture to exquisitely carved silverware, craftspeople and artists infused commonplace goods with unique motifs. Their creations were a seamless fusion of practicality and beauty, honoring both European tradition and New World inventions.

2. Academic Influence: The city developed become a center for scholarly and creative endeavors as a result of the College of William & Mary's existence. The college promoted a culture where art was valued, investigated, and discussed, which encouraged the emergence of numerous artistic trends.

3. Modern and contemporary art: Williamsburg embraced modern and contemporary creative movements in the 20th and 21st centuries. Avant-garde art became more accessible and

pervasive when galleries starting showing it and street art started decorating city walls.

Music and cultural festivals' effects

1. Traditional Songs: Early music in Williamsburg was greatly impacted by European settlers. The streets were filled with the sounds of folk songs, ballads, and hymns, many of which told stories of love, adversity, and hope. Mandolins, banjos, and fiddles became common musical instruments.

2. Jazz, Blues, and Beyond: The city's musical landscape grew over time. Jazz and blues were first performed in Williamsburg throughout the 20th century, drawing crowds from all around to the neighborhood's clubs and taverns.

3. Cultural Festivals: Williamsburg's calendar is jam-packed with events that honor its illustrious past and diverse population. The annual Colonial Williamsburg Festival transports you back in time with historical recreations, handcrafted items, and music from the era. As the city's musical preferences change, modern festivals highlight genres including rock, pop, and indie music.

4. International Influences: As numerous populations have moved in throughout the years, Williamsburg's cultural environment has benefited from international influences. The city has evolved into a melting pot of international cultures, with events ranging from Latin dance festivals to Asian art exhibitions.

To sum up, Williamsburg's artistic, musical, and cultural scene reflect its historical development. The city has accepted a wide range of expressions, from the old to the modern, making it a destination for musicians, artists, and culture buffs alike. Its celebrations of the past and artistic movements open the door for a future filled with innovation and cultural discovery.

Chapter 15: Education and Institutions

One of Williamsburg's most distinguishing characteristics is its academic history. The city has always been a center of study, establishing the standard for academic endeavors in the area. The institutions based in Williamsburg have been essential in shaping national narratives about research and education, as well as local ones.

History of Important Educational Facilities

The College of William & Mary is the second-oldest institution of higher study in the United States, having been established in 1693. It was funded by King William III and Queen Mary II of England and began as a little project before gaining popularity. Its distinguished alumni, which include former presidents of the United States, justices of the Supreme Court, and other noteworthy people, attest to its intellectual quality. The college's Sir Christopher Wren Building is the country's oldest college structure still in operation.

2. Bruton Heights School: During the 20th century's struggle with segregation, Williamsburg's African-American pupils looked to Bruton Heights School as a model of excellence in education. From its founding in the late 1940s until desegregation in the late 1960s, it provided services to the Black community. It has been transformed into a Colonial Williamsburg office, research, and instructional center and now stands as a symbol of tenacity and perseverance.

The City's Position in Research and Education

1. Intellectual Hub: Williamsburg was positioned as an intellectual powerhouse from the start by the College of William & Mary. Its founding attracted academics and intellectuals from all over, sparking discussions, debates, and intellectual undertakings that would influence the fundamental foundation of American thought.

2. Academic Research: Williamsburg institutions have always been at the forefront of academic research. In particular, the College of William & Mary has achieved important advances in a variety of subject areas, including environmental science, law, physics, and history. Its scientific institutions, such as the Virginia Institute of Marine Science, have significantly contributed to expanding human knowledge.

3. Community and academia: Williamsburg promoted a culture of lifelong learning among its community outside of official institutions. Every part of the city was filled with a spirit of study thanks to libraries, public lectures, seminars, and community classes.

4. Contemporary Educational Innovations: Williamsburg's educational philosophy evolved along with the rest of the globe. The city made sure that its educational institutions stayed current and cutting-edge by embracing technology, diversifying curricula, and creating international collaborations.

In conclusion, Williamsburg's dedication to education is ingrained in its culture. In addition to imparting information, its institutions have promoted the virtues of innovation, critical thinking, and societal contribution. Its status as a true fortress of learning, reflecting its past and illuminating the way for future generations, is underscored by the city's significance in academics and research.

Chapter 16: Natural Disasters and Their Impact

Like other older communities, Williamsburg has experienced its share of natural disasters. These situations have put the city's spirit, resiliency, and residents' fortitude to the test. Nevertheless, each difficulty has provided Williamsburg with a chance to unite, rebuild, and come out on top.

Important Events

1. Floods: The city has occasionally experienced flooding as a result of its proximity to waterways, particularly the James and York rivers. Over the years, Williamsburg has struggled with flooded streets and damaged infrastructure, particularly during times of intense rain or after hurricanes.

2. Fires: According to historical sources, Williamsburg has occasionally been in danger from fires. The most notable was the fire in 1705, which obliterated a sizable chunk of the town. Fires not only posed immediate risks, but also ran the risk of destroying priceless historical buildings.

3. Hurricanes: Because Williamsburg is situated in the Mid-Atlantic region, it occasionally experiences hurricanes and tropical storms. Along with the winds and rainfall, these natural disasters also carry the risk of lengthy power outages and infrastructure damage.

4. Earthquakes: Williamsburg has experienced earthquake tremors, albeit they are not as frequent as in some other areas.

These incidents, however usually of a minor magnitude, serve as a reminder of nature's erratic force.

The City's Recovery and Will to Survive

1. Community Spirit: Williamsburg's residents have consistently shown amazing togetherness in the face of tragedy. The city's pillars during tough times have been neighbors assisting neighbors, volunteer groups organizing resources, and a general sense of oneness.

2. Infrastructure Reinforcement: The city has prioritized evaluating and strengthening its infrastructure following each severe natural disaster. By taking these measures, whether it be repairing historic structures after fires or enhancing drainage systems after floods, Williamsburg will be better equipped to face new difficulties.

3. Disaster Preparedness: Williamsburg has created extensive preparations for disaster preparedness after studying historical incidents. These strategies, along with frequent drills and community awareness campaigns, are meant to reduce harm and promote a speedy recovery.

4. Historical Preservation: Due to Williamsburg's extensive historical legacy, preservation efforts have been of utmost importance. After calamities, groups like Colonial Williamsburg Foundation have been instrumental in maintaining and rebuilding historical sites.

In conclusion, Williamsburg unquestionably bears the scars of nature. Williamsburg's resilience is demonstrated by its residents' tenacity and the city's proactive rehabilitation and readiness efforts. Each catastrophe has not only been a trying time, but also a chapter of resilience, cohesion, and rejuvenation.

Chapter 17: Sports and Recreation

Any city's vitality is frequently reflected in how its citizens enjoy sports and leisure time. Sports and recreation have played a special role in cultivating talent, establishing community, and promoting health and wellness in Williamsburg, a city with rich historical traditions.

Williamsburg, Virginia, Sports Teams and Athletes Throughout History

1. The Origins of Sports: Early immigrants in Williamsburg enjoyed playing traditional English sports like cricket, rugby, and horseshoes, which over time grew to be an important part of social events. These developed over time, laying the way for current sports like football, basketball, and baseball.

2. Local Teams: Despite the absence of big league professional teams in Williamsburg, the city has produced a number of fiercely competitive local teams that have made a lasting impression on state championships. For instance, The College of William & Mary has a storied history in athletics, with teams participating in NCAA Division I. Particularly its football and basketball teams have seen success at times, garnering regional and international notice.

3. Notable Athletes: A number of Williamsburg-born athletes have gone on to achieve success at the state, national, and even worldwide levels. These neighborhood role models have evolved into motivational icons for the city's aspiring athletes. The list of

such athletes is lengthy, but examples include William & Mary football players who joined the NFL or local baseball players selected by MLB.

Recreational Spaces: What They Mean

1. Parks and Green Spaces: Williamsburg is littered with a lot of parks and green spaces, which are all great places for locals to unwind, play, or just take in the scenery. With its lovely reservoir, Waller Mill Park provides boating, fishing, and scenic walks. Similar to this, the community-run playground Kidsburg offers a secure setting for kids to play and families to connect.

2. Trails and Natural Reserves: Williamsburg has a wide selection of trails, from the tranquil Greensprings Interpretive Trail to the more difficult hiking trails in adjacent preserves, for individuals who enjoy outdoor activities. These trails serve as a resource for pleasure as well as environmental education and protection.

3. Colonial Williamsburg: Colonial Williamsburg is primarily a historical monument, but it also doubles as a sizable recreation area. Its large lawns hold neighborhood gatherings, customary games, and even colonial-era sports, providing a distinctive fusion of history and enjoyment.

4. Golf courses: Many Williamsburg residents hold a special place in their hearts for the game of golf. Numerous top-notch golf courses are located throughout the city, drawing both local and out-of-town players.

In essence, recreation and sports are an important part of Williamsburg's culture, not just passtimes. They show how the city has changed, how it embraces modernization while maintaining a strong connection to heritage, and how it is dedicated to cultivating a sense of community and well-being. These activities, whether supporting a neighborhood team or enjoying a leisurely stroll through a park, are windows into Williamsburg and its people.

Chapter 18: Modern Challenges and Innovations

As the 21st century progressed, Williamsburg faced a variety of contemporary difficulties that put its residents' foresight, adaptation, and tenacity to the test. However, the city's dedication to securing a sustainable future and utilizing technology meant that these difficulties also served as catalysts for truly exceptional breakthroughs.

Environmental Concerns and Sustainable Development Programs

1. Recognizing Environmental Footprints: Concerns regarding carbon footprints, waste management, water conservation, and habitat destruction arose as Williamsburg's urbanization grew. Williamsburg took aggressive measures to evaluate and lessen its environmental impact when climate change became a global issue.

2. Sustainable Williamsburg: Several initiatives were started that address a range of topics.

Green building: Promoting the use of materials and designs that are less energy-intensive throughout construction projects.

Waste management: Supporting initiatives for composting, recycling, and waste reduction with the goal of drastically reducing landfill waste.

Investing in environmentally friendly public transportation can help cut down on vehicle emissions.

Water conservation includes creating methods for collecting rainwater, reusing graywater, and ensuring the cleanliness of nearby waterways.

3. Community Involvement: Williamsburg's environmental activities were heavily reliant on the participation of its residents. Every person has a stake in the city's green future thanks to awareness campaigns, workshops, and community-led conservation initiatives.

Technological Progress having its origin in Williamsburg, Virginia

1. The Academic Catalyst: As a center of innovation, the College of William & Mary played a crucial role. Its research divisions and partnerships with the tech sector gave rise to innovations in domains like data analytics and sustainable energy sources.

2. Technology-based startups: Williamsburg had a boom in this sector, particularly in the fields of software development, biotechnology, and green technology. The city was a desirable headquarters for businesses due to its blend of old-world elegance and contemporary conveniences.

3. Smart City Initiatives: Williamsburg started the process of becoming a smart city by utilizing technological breakthroughs. The quality of life for citizens was improved with IoT (Internet

of Things) integrations in public utilities, AI-driven traffic management, and digitally upgraded municipal services.

4. Heritage Preservation: Technology was also used to preserve Williamsburg's extensive history, creating a lovely union of the old and the new. Residents and visitors were able to experience the city's past in engaging new ways thanks to augmented reality tours, digital archiving, and 3D reconstructions.

Williamsburg demonstrated its innovative spirit by addressing its contemporary problems head-on and converting possible setbacks into chances for development. The city's simultaneous dedication to sustainability and technological advancement presents a positive image of its future, one in which the rich lessons of the past and the opportunities of the future smoothly converge.

Chapter 19: Conclusion

Williamsburg, Virginia, where the old and new coexist in peaceful resonance, stands as a tribute to the ageless American story. It continues to be a legendary city as we move deeper into the twenty-first century, with every brick and stone whispering tales of the past even as its streets hum with the vitality of the future.

The Prospects for Williamsburg, Virginia in the Future

The horizon of the metropolis shimmers with promise. Williamsburg is now positioned as both a keeper of the past and a leader in cutting-edge technology thanks to investments in sustainable practices. It is positioned to continue serving as a center of culture, business, and community with sustained dedication to education, innovation, and inclusion.

At the start of a new period, Williamsburg's development does not automatically come to an end. It resides in its capacity to transform, adapt, and imagine a better future. Williamsburg's community's commitment to embracing change while upholding its historical origins guarantees that its story will continue to inspire for centuries to come.

Analysis of Its Development and Importance in the Tapestry of American History

The voyage of Williamsburg is nothing short of miraculous. The city has been both a participant and a significant witness in the grand theater of American history since its founding, when native tribes and early settlers interacted, through its crucial role in the revolutionary and civil war eras, and into its ongoing expansion and transformation.

Its importance to the history of the country is unrivaled. Williamsburg serves as a microcosm of America as a whole because it was the birthplace of revolutionary ideas, the scene of battles that determined the course of the country, and a living history museum.

Chapter 20: Must-See Locations

1. Colonial Williamsburg: Serving as the city's focal point, Colonial Williamsburg whisks visitors away to the 18th century. One can actually experience the life and spirit of America's colonial era thanks to its painstakingly rebuilt buildings, costumed interpreters, and bustling market squares.

2. The Governor's Palace: Formerly the Royal Governors of the Colony of Virginia's principal house, this imposing building is a marvel of colonial design, complete with beautiful gardens and elaborate interiors.

3. The College of William & Mary: The College of William & Mary is the second-oldest higher education institution in America. Its magnificent campus is rich in academic renown and history. Particularly impressive from an architectural standpoint is the Sir Christopher Wren Building.

4. Jamestown Settlement: This living history museum tells the tale of America's first permanent English colony and is within a short drive from Williamsburg. A multisensory voyage into the early 1600s is provided by realistic recreations of the ships, the fort, and the Powhatan settlement.

5. Busch Gardens: If you're looking for excitement and fun, Busch Gardens has a thrilling selection of roller coasters, live performances, and themed attractions that combine European ambiance with daring exhilaration.

The Abby Aldrich Rockefeller Folk Art Museum is a celebration of American folk art and is home to an extraordinary collection of fabrics, decorative objects, paintings, and sculptures that capture the inventiveness of the country's first artists.

7. Visit Historic Jamestown and stroll through the area where the first English settlers arrived in 1607. Visitors to the location can take archaeological excursions to see the ongoing digs that are helping to piece together the history of early America.

8. Water Country USA: Virginia's largest water park offers a splash-filled adventure and is a great place for family outings with its abundance of slides, wave pools, and lazy rivers.

9. DeWitt Wallace Decorative Arts Museum: Showcasing furniture, metalwork, pottery, and other items from the 17th, 18th, and 19th centuries, the museum is home to a wide variety of British and American antiquities.

10. Williamsburg Winery: A stop at Williamsburg Winery is a must for wine connoisseurs. The winery, which is tucked away in a luscious vineyard, provides tours, tastings, and insights into the finer points of winemaking.

Don't miss out!

Visit the website below and you can sign up to receive emails whenever Henry Church publishes a new book. There's no charge and no obligation.

https://books2read.com/r/B-A-GDIAB-UYRNC

BOOKS 2 READ

Connecting independent readers to independent writers.

Also by Henry Church

American Cities History Guidebook Series
Charlottesville, Virginia: Historical Guide for Travelers
Williamsburg, Virginia: Historical Guide for Travelers
Richmond, Virginia: Historical Guide for Travelers
Norfolk & Virginia Beach: Historical Guide for Travelers
Winchester, Virginia: Historical Guide for Travelers
Baltimore, Maryland: Historical Guide for Travelers
Dover, Delaware: Historical Guide for Travelers
Arlington, Virginia: Historical Guide for Travelers

About the Publisher

Fiel LLC is dedicated to providing high-quality content at affordable prices, utilizing state-of-the-art processes and advanced content generation systems to ensure a superior reading experience. All books published by Fiel LLC are for entertainment purposes only. Fiel LLC authors use pen names and are not experts in any field, so no content should be taken as financial, medical, legal, or professional advice. All information provided is subject to change, and readers are encouraged to verify the latest details through their own research.